Tahira has been knitting for over 20 years and writing patterns since 2010. This is her first book in which she has created visibly beautiful flowers and vases. She has created these easy-to-follow patterns from beginner level to advanced knitter with basic stitches that are easy to follow. She gives classes for beginners to learn knitting in the local community.

I would like to dedicate this book to my daughter Aneela, who has inspired me with her creativity and inspiration.

Tahira Ahmed

10 FLOWER AND VASE KNITTING PATTERNS

AUSTIN MACAULEY PUBLISHERS™
LONDON • CAMBRIDGE • NEW YORK • SHARJAH

Copyright © Tahira Ahmed 2023

The right of Tahira Ahmed to be identified as author of this work has been asserted by the author in accordance with sections 77 and 78 of the Copyright, Designs and Patents Act 1988.

All rights reserved. No part of this publication may be reproduced, stored in a retrieval system, or transmitted in any form or by any means, electronic, mechanical, photocopying, recording, or otherwise, without the prior permission of the publishers.

Any person who commits any unauthorized act in relation to this publication may be liable to criminal prosecution and civil claims for damages.

A CIP catalogue record for this title is available from the British Library.

ISBN 9781398472365 (Paperback)
ISBN 9781398472372 (ePub e-book)

www.austinmacauley.com

First Published 2023
Austin Macauley Publishers Ltd®
1 Canada Square
Canary Wharf
London
E14 5AA

Table of Contents

Chapter 1: Flower and Vase 1	9
Chapter 2: Flower and Vase 2	14
Chapter 3: Flower and Vase 3	20
Chapter 4: Flower and Vase 4	25
Chapter 5: Flower and Vase 5	33
Chapter 6: Flower and Vase 6	41
Chapter 7: Flower and Vase 7	48
Chapter 8: Flower and Vase 8	55
Chapter 9: Flower and Vase 9	61
Chapter 10: Flower and Vase 10	67

Chapter 1
Flower and Vase 1

6" Tall:

For this project, you will need
3 ¼ Knitting needles
5 lengths of 12-inch pipe cleaners, 4 cuts into 4-inch lengths, 1 cut in half for base

Handful of toy stuffing
Length of ribbon
4 cm diameter round of cardboard

Abbreviations
K: knit, P: pearl
Inc: increase
Tog: together
sts: stitches
st-st: stocking stitch

To make vase
Cast on 30 stitches
R1 – Knit row
R2 – Pearl row
R3 – Knit row
R4 – Pearl row
R5 – Knit row
R6 – Pearl row
R7 – K1, K2tog to end
R8 – Pearl row
R9 – Knit Row
R10 – Pearl row
R11 – Knit row
R12 – Pearl row
R13 – Knit row
R14 – Pearl row
R15 – (k4 inc in next stitch), repeat till end (24sts)
R16 – Pearl row
R17 – Knit row
R18 – Pearl row

R19 – (K5, inc in next stitch) repeat until end (28sts)
R20 – Pearl row
R21 – Knit row
R22 – Pearl row
R23 – K4, Inc in next stitch, (K2 Inc in next stitch, repeat 6 times), k4, Inc next stitch (36sts)
R24 – Pearl row
R25 – Knit row
R26 – Pearl row
R27 – k4, k2tog, (K2, K2tog 6 times), K4, k2tog – (28sts)
R28 – Pearl row
R29 – Knit row
R30 – Pearl row
R31 – K3, K2tog, (K1, K2tog, 6 times), K3, K2 tog – (20sts)
R32 – Pearl row
R33 – Knit row
R34 – Pearl row
R35 – K3, K2tog repeat 4 times (16sts)
R36 – Knit row
R37 – Knit row
R38 – Knit row
R39 – K2tog, to end (8sts)
R40 – K2tog, to end (4sts)
R41 – Cut off wool and draw through the stitches sew upside of vase.

Cut out a 4 cm diameter round of cardboard to put in the base of the vase and stuff; making sure you don't overstuff.

For the stand at the base of the vase, tie 6-inch pipe cleaner into a circle and secure at the bottom of the vase.

Press a hole in the middle of the vase and put flowers in.

To make flowers:
Cast on 2 stitches
R1 – inc 3 stitches and cast off 3 stitches, k2
R2 – Pearl
R3 – inc 3 stitches and cast off 3 stitches, k2
R4 – pearl
R5 – inc 3 stitches and cast off 3 stitches, k2
R6 – Pearl
R7 – inc 3 stitches and cast off 3 stitches, k2
R8 – pearl
R9 – inc 3 stitches and cast off 5 stitches

Turn in the pipe cleaner at the top to make the middle of the flower and bottom. Sew the two sides of the flower and loosely sew around the middle of the flower; insert the pipe cleaner and pull wool, so it's tight against the pipe cleaner and secure around the back of flower.

Make 8 or 10 in different colours or as desired.

To make heart (make 2)
Cast on 1 stitch
R1 – K, inc 1 stitch, (2sts)
R2 – P
R3 – K inc into the 2sts (4sts)
R4 – P
R5 – K inc into the 2 and 3sts (6sts)
R6 – P
R7 – K inc into 2 and 5sts (8sts)

Row 8 – P
R9 – K inc into 2 and 7sts
(10sts)
R10 – P
R11 -K
R12 – P
R13 – K inc into 2 and 9st (12sts)
R14 – P6 stitches turn
R15 – K1, K2tog k3 (5sts)
R16 – P
R17 – K2tog, k1, K2 tog (3sts)
R18 – P2tog, p1
Cut off and slip thread through stitches
Re-join tread pearl to end
K1, K2 tog, k3 (5sts)
Next P
Next K2tog, k1, K2 tog (3sts)
Next P2tog, p1

Cut off and slip thread through stitches

Sew up edges leaving enough space to stuff; stuff and join seam.

Add a length of pipe cleaner to back and place in vase to make stem.

Knit 1 stitch until 7 inch long and fold in middle and attach pipe cleaner and embed in vase.

Finally tie ribbon around the top of the vase.

Chapter 2
Flower and Vase 2

15" Tall:

Flower and Vase 2

For this project, you will need

3 ¼ Knitting needles

3 ¼ Double pointed needles

100 g chunky 30% wool

2 ply wools, red and green

Toy stuffing
Length ribbon
Round of cardboard for inside base of vase: 5 cm diameter.
Pipe cleaner for outside base vase
French knitting tool
Wire for the flower stems

Abbreviations
K – Knit, P – Pearl
Inc – increase
Tog – together
St-st – stocking stitch
St/sts – Stitch / stitches

Vase
Row0 – Cast on 40s
Row1–10 – st-st, starting with knit row
Row11 – K2, K2tog – (30sts)
Row12–24 st-st
Row25 – K2, Inc in next stitch repeat to end – (40sts)
Row26–28 st-st
Row29 – K3, Inc in next stitch, repeat to end – (50sts)
Row30–38 st-st
Row39 – (K9, K2tog to end) K6 (46sts)
Row40–44 st-st
Row 45 – (K7, K2tog to end) k1(41sts)
Row46–50 st-st
Row51 – (K6, K2tog, repeat to end) k1 (36 sts)
Row52–54 st-st
Row 55 – (K5, K2tog, repeat to end) k1 (31sts)
Row56–59 st-st

Row60 – (K1, K2tog, repeat to end) (21sts)
Row61 – K
Row62 – K
Row63 – K
Row64 – K2tog(11sts)
Row65 – K2tog(6sts)

Cut of wool and draw through the stitches and sew up the two sides.

Cut out 5 cm diameter of cardboard to put in the base of the vase and stuff, making sure you don't overstuff.

Stand

French knitting tool or double pointed needles (cast on 4sts)

Create a stem 22 cm long. Join end together and attach to around bottom vase.

Press a hole in the middle of the vase and put flowers in.

Rose

Large petal (make 4)
Cast on 6 sts
Row1 – K
Row2 – P, increase in 1st and last st (8sts)
Row3 – Knit
Row4 – P, increase in 1st and last st (10sts)
Row5 – K
Row6 – P, increase in 1st and last st (12sts)
Row7 – K
Row8 – P
Row9 – K, K2tog at 1st and last st (10sts)
Row10 – P

Row11 – K
Row12 – P
Row13 – K, K2tog at 1st and last st (8sts)
Row14 – P
Row15 – K
Row16 – P, P2 tog at 1st and last st (6sts)
Row17 – K, K2tog at 1st and last st (4sts)
Cast off

Middle petal (make 3)

Cast on 6 sts
Row1 – K
Row2 – P
Row3 – K, increase in 1st and last st (8sts)
Row4 – P
Row5 – K
Row6 – P
Row7 – K, increase in 1st and last st (10sts)
Row8 – P
Row9 – K
Row10 – P, P2 tog at 1st and last st (8sts)
Row11 – K
Row12 – P
Row13 – K, K2tog at 1st and last st (6sts)
Row14 – P
Cast off

Inner petal (make 1)

Cast on 5 sts
Stocking stitch 13 rows
Cast off

Leaves (make 3)

Cast on 3 sts
Row1 – K
Row2 – K1, P1, K1
Row3 – inc1, K1, inc1 (5sts)
Row4 – K2, P1, K2
Row5 – inc1, k3, inc1 (7sts)
Row6 – K3, P1, K3
Row7 – Knit
Row8 – K3, P1, K3
Row9 – K2tog, k3, K2tog (5sts)
Row10 – K2, P1, K2
Row11 – K2tog, K1, K2tog (3sts)
Row12 – K1, P1, K1
Row13 – K3tog
Cast off

Stem (make 2)

For the stem, you will need a French knitting tool; create a green stem 20 and 15 cm long.

Take covered wire fold over at edges and pass through the stem, and then sew on to flower at the back.

Making up

Take middle petals and sew around rounded inner petal in a round circle overlapping petals. Then take large petals and sew around the middle petals in a round circle overlapping petals. Hold tightly and place a stitch 2 cm from bottom through the flower to the other side petal, then do same for the other side, leaving an indent in the petals.

Sew the three leaves around the base of flower, then attach the stem.

Chapter 3
Flower and Vase 3

Vase 5 ½ with flowers 13":

Flower and Vase 3

For this project, you will need

3 ¼ Knitting needles,

4 double-pointed knitting needles,

100 g chunky wool

Oddments of wool

Toy stuffing
Length ribbon
Round of cardboard for inside base of vase: 7.5 cm diameter
Pipe cleaner for outside base vase
French knitting tool
Wire for the flower stems
7 ½" each

Abbreviations
K – Knit, P – Pearl
Inc – increase
Tog – together
St-st – stocking stitch
St / sts – Stitch / stitches

Vase
Row0 – Cast on 70 sts
Row1–10 – starting with Knit row st st
Row11 – K5, K2tog to end (60sts)
Row12–24 St st
Row25 – K2, Inc 1 in next st (80sts)
Row26 – P
Row27 – K7, Inc 1 in next st (90sts)
Row28 – P
Row29 – K5, Inc 1 in next st (105sts)
Row30–44 – st st
Row45 – K5, K2tog to end (90sts)
Row46 – P
Row47 – K 7, K2tog to end (80sts)
Row48 – P
Row49 – K6, K2tog to end (70sts)

Row50–54 st st
Row55 – K5, K2tog to end (60sts)
Row57–60 – st st
Row61 – K2tog to end (30sts)
Row62 – K
Row63 – K
Row64 – K
Row65 – K
Row66 – K2tog to end (15sts)
Row67 – Knit
Row68 – K2tog to end, K1 (8sts)

Cut of wool and draw through the stitches and sew up the two sides.

Cut out 7.5 cm diameter of cardboard to put in the base of the vase and stuff, making sure you don't over stuff.

For the stand at the base of the vase, tie inch pipe cleaner into a circle and secure at the bottom of the vase or use French knitting tool or double pointed needles (cast on 4sts)

Create a stem 21 cm long.

Join end together and attach to around bottom vase.

Press a hole in the middle of the vase and put flowers in.

Daffodil

Petal (Knit 6 pieces)
Row 0 – Cast on 3sts
Row1 – knit
Row2 – Increase in 1st and last st (5sts)
Row3 – Knit Row4-Increase in 1st and last st (7st)
Row5–19 knit
Row20 – K 2tog, k3, K2tog (5sts)
Row21 – K 2tog, k1, K2tog (3sts)

Row22 – K3tog

Cast off.

Stitch petals overlapping each other in a round, slightly cup shape. Sew all petals at bottom slightly touching other petal.

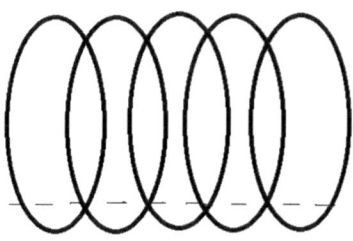

Bell

Knit on double pointed needles and split between 3.

Cast on 10

Row1–10 – knit

Row11 – increase in every stitch (20sts)

Row12 – K

Cast off

Sew the bottom to form round to place in middle flower petals.

Receptacle

Cast on 5 sts

Knit 30 rows (Garter stitch)

Cast off

Knit the side, then gather on side to form small round to attach to main stem.

Stem

Using French knitting doll knit 8-inch-long tube for main stem, tighten bottom and slip 8-inch wire in the tube, sew on receptacle. Stitch bell in middle of petals. Attach the receptacle to petals.

Leaf
Cast on 5sts
Row 1–10 knit
Row 11, K2, K2tog, K1
(3sts)
Row 12–15 – K
Row 16 – Cast off, K 3 tog.
Attach to stem.

Chapter 4
Flower and Vase 4

7 ½" Vase, 15 ½" with Flowers:

Flower and Vase 4

For this project, you will need

3¼ knitting needles

3¼ Double pointed needles 100 g chunky wool

Oddments red, yellow and green,

Toy stuffing

Length ribbon
Round of cardboard for inside base of vase: 6.5 cm diameter.
French knitting tool
Wire for the flower stems

Abbreviations

k – knit, p – pearl
Inc – increase
Tog – together
St-st – stocking stitch
St/sts – stitch/stitches

Vase

Row 0 cast on 60 sts
Row 1–10 starting with a knit row st-st
Row 11 – K4, K2tog to end (50sts)
Row 12–24 st-st
Row 25 – K9, Inc in next stitch to end (55sts)
Row 26–28 st-st
Row29 – K10, Inc in next stitch to end (60sts)
Row30–34 – st-st
Row35-K11, Inc in next stitch to end (65sts)
Row36–38-st-st
Row39 – K12, Inc in next stitch to end (70sts)
Row40–54 – st-st
Row55 – k12, K2tog to end (65sts)
Row56–60 – st-st
Row61 – K11, K2tog to end (60sts)
Row62–64 – st-st
Row65 – K10, K2 tog to end (55sts)
Row66–68 – st-st

Row69 – K9, K2tog to end (50sts)
Row70–74 – st-st
Row75 – K8, K2tog to end (45sts)
Row76–78 – st-st
Row79 – K7, K2tog to end (40sts)
Row80 – K
Row81 – K
Row82 – K2, K2tog (30sts)
Row83 – K
Row84 – K1, K2tog to end (20sts)
Row85 – K
Row86 – K2tog to end (10sts)

Cut of wool and draw through the stitches and sew up the two sides.

Making up

Cut out a 6.5 cm diameter of cardboard to put in the base of the vase and stuff, making sure you don't overstuff.

Stand

French knitting tool or double pointed needles (cast on 4sts).

Create a stem 26 cm long. Join end together and attach to around bottom vase.

Press a hole in the middle of the vase and put flowers in.

Flower
(Instruction to make one flower, make as many as desired)
Inner Part

Cast on 6 Sts
Row1–14 – st-st

(For 2 tones change colours on 13th row)
Cast off

Middle Part
Make 4 pieces
Cast on 8sts
Row1 – K
Row2 – P
Row3 – K, Inc in 1st and last st (10sts)
Row4 – P
Row5 – K
Row6 – P, Inc in 1st and last st (12sts)
Row7–12 – st-st
Row13 – K2 tog, K8, K2tog (10sts)
Row14 – P2tog, P6, P2tog (8sts)
Row15 – K (For 2 tone, change colour)
Row16 – P2tog, P4, P2tog (6sts)
Row17 – K
Row18 – P2tog, K2, P2tog (4sts)
Cast off.

Outer Part
Make 5 pieces
Cast on 10sts
Row1 – K
Row2 – P, Inc in 1st and last st(12sts)
Row3 – K, Inc in 1st and last st(14sts)
Row4 – P
Row5 – K, Inc in 1st and last st(16sts)
Row6–9 – st-st
Row10 – P2tog, P12, P2tog (14sts)

Row11 – K
Row12 – P2tog, P10, P2tog (12sts)
Row13 – K
Row14 – P2tog, P8, P2tog (10sts)
Row15 – K
Row16 – P2tog, P6, P2tog (8sts)
Row17 – K (For 2 tone, change colour)
Row18 – P2tog, K4, P2tog (6sts)
Row19 – K
Row20 – P2tog, P2, P2tog (4sts)
Cast off.

To make

Take middle petals and sew around rounded inner petal in a round circle overlapping petals.

Purl inside, purl outside.

Then take large petals and tack overlapping and sew around the middle petals in a round circle.

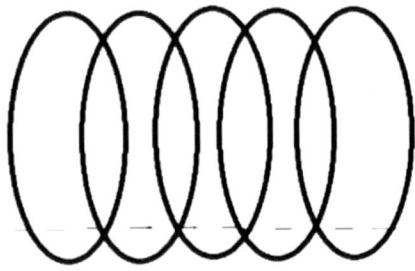

Hold tightly and place a stitch 1.5 cm from bottom through the flower on 2 sides to the other side.

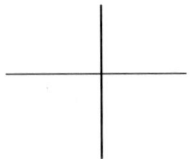

Base of Rose
Cast on 5 sts.
K 30 rows (Garter stitch).
Cast off.
Sew up at sides and gather one side to leave a small opening to sew on stem.

Stem (Make 1)
For the stem, you will need a French knitting tool.
Create a green stem 9 inch and 10 inch long.
Take covered wire fold over at edges and pass through the stem and then sew on to flower at the back.

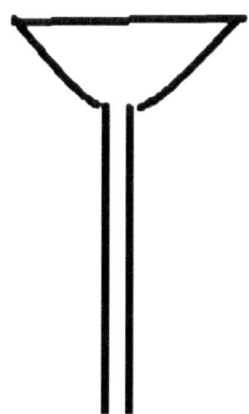

Base.

Leaf

Cast on 9sts
Row1 – K
Row2 – K4, P1, K4
Row3 – K
Row4 – K4, P1, K4
Row5 – K, Inc in 1st and last st (11sts)
Row6 – K5, P1, K5
Row7 – K, Inc in 1st and last st(13sts)
Row8 – K6, P1, K6
Row9 – K, Inc in 1st and last st(15sts)
Row10 – K7, P1, K7
Row11 – K
Row12 – K7, P1, K7
Row13 – K2tog, K11, K2tog (13sts)
Row14 – K6, P1, K6

Row15 – K
Row16 – K6, P1, K6
Row17 – K2tog, K9, K2tog (11sts)
Row18 – K5, P1, K5
Row19 – K2tog, K7, K2tog (9sts)
Row20 – K4, P1, K4
Row21 – K2tog, K5, K2tog (7sts)
Row22 – K3, P1, K3
Row23 – K2tog, K3, K2tog (5sts)
Row24 – K2, P1, K2
Row25 – K2tog, K1, K2tog (3sts)
Row26 – K2tog, K1 (2sts)
Row27 – K2tog

Attach to stem.

Chapter 5
Flower and Vase 5

Vase 7" with Flowers 15":

Flower and vase 5

For this project, you will need:

3 ¼ knitting needles

100 g chunky wool Oddments of wool, red and green

Double pointed needles 3 ¼

Toy stuffing

Length ribbon
Round of cardboard for inside base of vase: 6.5 cm diameter.
French knitting tool
Covered wire for the flower stems

Abbreviations

K – Knit, P – Pearl
Inc – increase
Tog – together
St-st – stocking stitch
Sts – Stitches

Flower

Large Petal (make 10)
Cast on 10sts
R1–4 – st-st starting with k row
R5, inc 1st and last st (12sts)
R6–10 st-st
R11, inc 1st and last st (14sts)
R12–16 st-st
R17 – K2tog, K10, K2tog(12sts)
R18 – P
R19 – K2tog, K8, K2tog(10sts)
R20–22 – st-st
R23 – K2tog, K6, K2tog (8sts)
R24 – P
R25, K2tog, K4, K2tog(6sts)
R26–28 – st-st
R29 – K2tog, K2, K2tog (4sts)
R30 – cast off

Middle Petal (make 4)

Cast on 8 sts
R1–9 – st-st starting with k row
R10 – Inc 1st and Last st (10sts)
R11–18 – st-st
R19 – K2tog, K6, K2tog (8sts)
R20–22 – st-st
R23 – K2tog, K4, K2tog (6sts)
R24–26 – st-st
R25 – cast off

Inner Petal (make 1)

Cast on 6sts R1–24, st-st, staring with K row.
Cast off.
Take inner part and fold.
Take the middle part petals and place around, securing in a square. Take the outer part and place petals overlapping each other and secure with a seam on the bottom. Then place around the middle part and secure. Take needle and secure 1 cm from the bottom rose through the rose at both sides.

Take middle petals and sew around rounded inner petal in a round circle overlapping petals.

Then take 5 large petals and tack overlapping and sew around the middle petals in a round circle.

Do the same for last 5 petals.

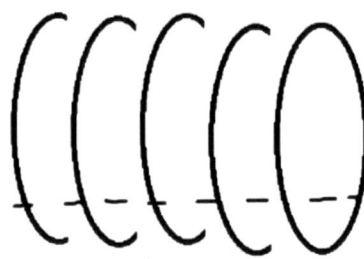

Hold tightly and place a stitch 2 cm from bottom through the flower on 2 sides to the other side.

Blade of Grass
Cast on 6sts
R1–29 – st-st
R30 – K2, K2tog, K2 (5sts)
R31–34 – st-st
R35 – K2, K2tog, K1 (4sts)
R36–38 – st-st

R39 – K1, K2tog, K1 (3sts)
R40–42 – st-st
R43 – K1, K2tog (2sts)
R44 – K
R45 – cast off

Base of Rose (make 1)
Cast on 10sts (Garter st)
R1–40 st-st, starting with Row

Grass stems (make 3)
K1st, 6 inch long

Leaf (make 2)
Cast on 9sts
R1 – K
R2 – K4, P1, K4
R3 – K
R4 – K4, P1, K4
R5 – K, Inc in 1st and last st(11sts)
R6 – K5, P1, K5
R7 – K, Inc in 1st and last st(13sts)
R8 – K6, P1, K6
R9 – K, Inc in 1st and last st(15sts)
R10 – K7, P1, K7
R11 – K
R12 – K7, P1, K7
R13 – K2tog, K11, K2tog(13sts)
R14 – K6, P1, K6
R15 – K
R16 – K6, P1, K6

R17 – K2tog, K9, K2tog (11sts)
R18 – K5, P1, K5
R19 – K2tog, K7, K2tog (9sts)
R20 – K4, P1, K4
R21 – K2tog, K5, K2tog (7sts)
R22 – K3, P1, K3
R23 – K2tog, K3, K2tog (5sts)
R24 – K2, P1, K2
R25 – K2tog, K1, K2tog (3sts)
R26 – K2tog, K1 (2sts) R27-K2tog

Attach leaf to stem attach to the flower stem; attach 2nd leaf to stem.

Stem for flower (make 1)

For the stem, you will need a French knitting tool or double pointed needles (cast on 4sts).

Create a green stem 10 inch long.

Take covered wire fold over at edges and pass through the stem, and then sew on base and attach flower at the back

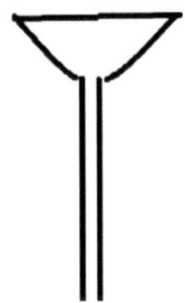

Vase

Cast on 60 sts

R1–10 starting with a k row – st-st

R11 – K4, K2 tog to end (50sts)
R12–24 – st-st
R25 – K9, Inc in next stitch to end (55sts)
R26–28 – st-st
R29 – K10, Inc in next stitch to end (60sts)
R30–34 – st-st
R35 – K11, Inc in next stitch to end (65sts)
R36–38 – st-st
R39 – K12, Inc in next stitch to end (70sts)
R40–54 – st-st
R55 – K12, K2tog to end (65sts)
R56–60 – st-st
R61 – K11, K2tog to end(60sts)
R62–64, st-st
R65 – K10, K2 tog to end (55sts)
Row66–68 – st-st
R69 – K9, K2tog to end (50sts)
R70–74 – st-st
R75 – K8, K2tog to end(45sts)
R76–78 – st-st
R 79 – K7, K2tog to end
(40sts)
R80 – K
R81 – K
R82 – K2, K2tog (30sts)
R 83 – K
R 84 – K1, K2tog to end(20sts)
R 85 – K
R 86 – K2tog to end (10sts) Cut of wool and draw through the stitches, and sew up the two sides.

Making up

Cut out a 6.5 cm diameter of cardboard to put in the base of the vase and stuff, making sure you don't overstuff.

At the bottom of the vase, press a hole in the middle of the vase and put flowers in.

Stand

French knitting tool or double pointed needles (cast on 4sts).

Create a stem 16.5 inch long.

Join end together and attach to around bottom vase.

Chapter 6
Flower and Vase 6

Height 16 inch:

For this project, you will need, 6 mm, 3¾ mm knitting needles
3 ¼ pointed knitting needles
Or French knitting tool. 1–100 g ball chunky wool for vase
Oddments of wool for flowers

Toy stuffing
Round of cardboard for bottom vase
Covered wire for stems.

Abbreviations

K – knit, P – pearl
Inc – increase
Tog – together
sts – stitches
st-st – stocking stitch
yo – yarn over needle
*– times

Outer Petals (Make 5)

Cast on 10 sts (size 6 needle)
R1 – K
R2 – K, K1, inc in 8 sts, K1 (18sts)
R3 – P
R4 – K
R5 – P
R6 – K
R7 – P
R8 – K, K1, (K2, K2tog, 4*)
K1 – (14sts)
R9 – P
R10 – K, K1, (K1, K2tog 4*)
K1 – (10sts)
R11 – P
R12 – K1 (K2tog, 4*) K1, (6sts)
R13 – (P2tog 3*), (3sts)
R14 – (K3tog), (1sts)

R15 – cast off

Middle section of Flower
(Make 5)
Cast on 8sts (size 6 needle)
R1 – K
R2 – K, K1 inc in next 6sts, K1 – (12sts)
R3 – P
R4 – K
R5 – P
R6 – K, K1, K2tog to end (8sts)
R7 – P
R8 – K, (K2tog to end) (4sts)
R9 – P, (P2tog to end) (2sts) R10-K2tog (1sts)
Cast off.

Centre flower (Make 1)
Cast on 8sts (size 6 needle)
R1   K
R2 – P
R3 – K
R4 – P, P2tog (4sts)
R5 – K, K2tog (2sts)
R6 – P, P2tog (1sts)
Cast off.

Back of flower
Cast on 8sts
Knit 20 rows garter st

Stem

Double pointed needles 3 ¼.

Knit stem 10-inch-long or to preference of arrangement of flowers.

Place covered wire through the stem.

Make up of flower.

Knit all pieces.

Sew the petals. Then place the back seam in the middle and fold the petal in half and place a stitch to hold at bottom.

Place the middle pieces around the center piece. Then place the outer petals around the middle petals. Place a few stitches 1 cm up through the base of flower and tighten, making a bottom for the base of flower.

Sew the base of flower at the side and tack the bottom and pull to form a tight hole.

Attach to stem, then attach to flower.

Vase

Row0 cast on 60 sts

Row1–10 – starting with a knit row st-st

Row11 – K4, K2tog to end (50sts)

Row12–24 – st-st

Row25 – K9, Inc in next stitch to end (55sts)

Row26–28 – st-st

Row29 – K10, Inc in next stitch to end (60sts)

Row30–34 – st-st

Row35 – k11, Inc in next stitch to end (65sts)

Row36–38 – st-st

Row39 – K12, Inc in next stitch to end (70sts)

Row40–54 – st-st

Row55 – k12, K2tog to end (65sts)
Row56–60 – st-st
Row61 – K11, K2tog to end (60sts)
Row62–64 – st-st
Row65 – K10, K2 tog to end (55sts)
Row66–68 st-st
Row69 – K9, K2tog to end (50sts)
Row70–74 – st-st
Row75 – K8, K2tog to end (45sts)
Row76–78 – st-st
Row79 – K7, K2tog to end(40sts)
Row80 – K
Row81 – K
Row82 – K2, K2tog (30sts)
Row83 – K
Row84 – K1, K2tog to end(20sts)
Row85 – K
Row86 – K2tog to end (10sts)

Cut of wool and draw through the stitches and sew up the two sides.

Making up

Cut out a 6.5 cm diameter of cardboard to put in the base of the vase and stuff, making sure you don't overstuff.

Stand

French knitting tool or double pointed needles (cast on 4sts).

Create a stem 26 cm long.

Join end together and attach to around bottom vase.

Press a hole in the middle of the vase and put flowers in.

Vase decoration

Cast on 40sts (size 6 needle)

R1 – K

R2 – K, K1, (yo, K2tog to end) K1

R3 – P

R4 – K, K1, (yo, K2tog to end) K1

R5 – P

R6 – K, Co 6sts at start of row, K1, (yo, K2tog to end) K1 (34sts)

R7 – P, Co 6sts at start of row, P1, (yo, P2tog to end) P1 (28sts)

R8 – K, Co 4sts at start of row, K1, (yo, K2tog to end) K1 (24sts)

R9 – P, Co 6sts at start of row, P1, (yo, P2tog to end) P1 (20sts)

R10 – K

R11 – P

R12 – K, Co 2sts at start of row, K1, (yo, K2tog to end) K1 (18sts)

R13 – P, Co 2sts at start of row, P1, (yo, P2tog to end) P1 (16sts)

R14 – K, Co 2sts at start of row, K1, (yo, K2tog to end) K1 (14sts)

R13 – P, Co 2sts at start of row, P1, (yo, P2tog to end) P1 (12sts)

R15 – K, Co 2sts at start of row, K1, (yo, K2tog to end) K1 (10sts)

R16 – P Co 2sts at start of row, P1, (yo, P2tog to end) P1 (8sts)

R17 – K, Co 2sts at start of row, K1, (yo, K2tog to end) K1 (6sts)

R18 – P Co 2sts at start of row, P1, (yo, P2tog to end) P1 (4sts)

R19 – K, K2 tog twice

R20 – cast off

Attach around neck of vase and stitch sides together.

Chapter 7
Flower and Vase 7

9" Tall:

Flower and Vase 7

3 ¼ Knitting Needles end (40sts)

Oddments of 2 ply wool R20–22 st-st

French knitting tool or 3 ¼ double pointed Knitting needles

(12 Inch pipe cleaners cut in half for stems of flower) Round of cardboard for base of flowerpot 5.5 cm diameter circle
Toy stuffing

Abbreviation

Yo – yarn over, wrap thread around needle
Sts – stitches
St – stitch
*– times
Tog – together

Vase

3 ¼ Knitting Needles Cast on 40 sts
R1 – starting with Knit – to row 10, st-st
R11 – K3, K2 tog to end, (32sts)
R12–18 – st-st
R19 – K3 Inc in next stitch to end (40sts)
R20–22 – st-st
R23 – K3 Inc next stitch, repeat to end, (50sts)
R24–26 – st-st
R27 – K9, Inc in next st, repeat to end (55 sts)
R28–30 – st-st
R31 – K3, K2tog to end (44sts)
R32–34 – st-st
R35 – K3, K2tog to end, K4(36sts)
R36–38 – st-st
R39 – K4, K2tog to end (30sts)
R40–42 – st-st
R43 – K3, K2tog to end(24sts)
R44 – K row
R45 – Knit row

R46 – Knit row
R47 – Knit row
R48 – K2, K2 tog to end, (18sts)
R49 – K2 tog, (9sts)
R50 – K2tog 4*, K1

Sew up sides and place 5.5 cm diameters round of cardboard in vase before stuffing. Stuff well to point of creating shape of vase.

Base of vase
Cast on 4sts

Using French knitting tool or double pointed needle; knit 19 cm long; attach to bottom of vase.

Vase Decoration
3 1/4 Knitting needles

Cast on 40 sts
R1 – K
R2 – P
R3 – Cast off 10 st at beg, K to end
R4 – Cast of 10st at beg, P to end
R5 – K2 tog, (yo, K2tog to end) K2tog (18sts)
R6 – K1, (yo, K2tog to end) K1
R7 – K2 tog, (yo, K2tog to end) K2tog(16sts)
R8 – K1, (yo, K2tog to end) K1
R9 – K2 tog, (yo, K2tog to end) K2tog(14sts)
R10 – K1, (yo, K2tog to end) K1
R11 – K2 tog, (yo, K2tog to end) K2tog(12sts)
R12 – K1, (yo, K2tog to end) K1
R13 – K2 tog, (yo, K2tog to end) K2tog(10sts)

R14 – K1, (yo, K2tog to end) K1
R15 – K2 tog, (yo, K2tog to end) K2tog(8sts)
R16 – K1, (yo, K2tog to end) K1
R17 – K2 tog, (yo, K2tog to end) K2tog(6sts)
R18 – K1, (yo, K2tog to end) K1
R19 – K2 tog, (yo, K2tog to end) K2tog(4sts)
R20 – K1, (yo, K2tog to end) K1
R21 – K2tog to end(2sts)
R22 – K2tog (1st)
R23 cast off

Attach around top of vase.

Take pipe cleaner and sew through flower.

Flowers
Cast on 4 st
Using French Knitting tool or double pointed needles, Knit 35 cm long.

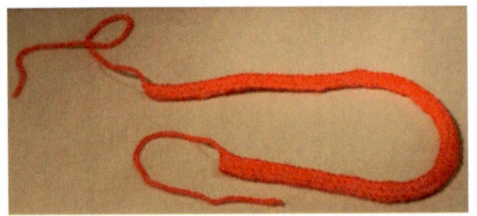

Gather on a knitting needle

Stitch the bottom of flower

Sew the two open sides together

Take Pipe cleaner and sew through flower

Secure at back, by twisting it

Grass

Brown or green wool

Knit 5 ½ stem.

Fold pipe cleaner at top and bottom

Use 6-inch pipe cleaner. Then push through the stem and sew at top and bottom.

This creates the grass.

To make up gather all flowers and grass and

Tie with a bit of wool and place in vase.

Chapter 8
Flower and Vase 8

6" Tall:

For this project, you will need:
3¾ mm knitting needles; 3¾ pointed knitting needles
Or French knitting tool. 1–100 g ball chunky wool for vase
Oddments of wool for flowers

Toy stuffing
Round of cardboard for bottom vase
Green pipe cleaners for stems
Ribbon

Abbreviations:

K – knit
P – pearl
Inc – increase
Tog – together
sts – stitches
st-st – stocking stitch
yo – yarn over needle
*– times

Flower

Cast on 3st
R1 – K, Inc 1st and 3rd stitch (5st)
R2 – P
R3 – K, Inc 1st and 3rd stitch (7st)
R4 – P
R5 – K
R6 – P
R7 – K-cast of beg and end row (5st)
R8 – P
R9 – K, cast of beg and end row(3st)
R10 – P
Repeat rows 1–10 9 times

To make up flower:

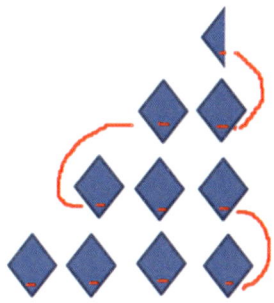

Fold first petal in half and stitch at bottom.

Stitch the second and third petal and wrap around first petal.

Stitch 4, 5 and 6 petals and wrap around 2nd and 3rd petal; secure.

Stitch 7, 8, 9 and 10 petals and wrap around 4, 5 and 6 petals and secure.

Leaf
Cast on 3sts.
R1 – K
R2 – K

R3 – Inc 1st and last st (5sts)
R4 – K
R5 – Inc 1st and last st (7sts)
R6 – K
R7 – K
R8 – K
R9 – Cast of 1 st and last st (5sts)
R10 – K
R11 – Cast of 1 st and last st (3sts)
R12 – K
R13 – Cast of first sts (2sts)
R14 – Knit tog (1 st)
R15 – Cast of
Attach leaf to flower

Attach stem to flower:

Take pipe cleaner and put through large needle and sew through flower base. Secure at back by twisting it.

Vase
To make vase:
Cast on 30 stitches
R1 – Knit row

R2 – Pearl row
R3 – Knit row
R4 – Pearl row
R5 – Knit row
R6 – Pearl row
R7 – K1, K2tog to end (20sts)
R8 – Pearl row
R9 – Knit Row
R10 – Pearl row
R11 – Knit row
R12 – Pearl row
R13 – Knit row
R14 – pearl row
R15 – (inc in every 2nd stitch), repeat till end (30sts)
R16 – Pearl row
R17 – Knit row (inc in every 3rd stitch), repeat till end (40sts)
R18 – Pearl row
R19 – Knit row (inc in every 4th stitch), repeat till end (50sts)
R20 – Pearl row
R21 – Knit row
R22 – pearl row
R23 – K3, K2tog to end (40sts)
R24 – Pearl row
R25 – K2, K2tog to end (30sts)
R26 – Pearl row
R27 – Knit row
R28 – Pearl row
R29 – Knit row
R30 – Pearl row
R31 – K1, K2tog to end (20sts)
R32 – Knit row

R33 – Knit row

R34 – Knit row

R35 – K2tog, to end (10sts)

R36 – K2tog, to end (5sts)

R37 – Cut off wool and draw through the stitches sew upside of vase.

Cut out a 4 cm diameter round of cardboard to put in the base of the vase and stuff, making sure you don't overstuff.

Stand

French knitting tool or double pointed needles (cast on 4sts).

Create a stem 17 cm long.

Join end together and attach to around bottom vase.

Chapter 9
Flower and Vase 9

6-inch vase with 13-inch flower:

For this project, you will need:

3 ¼ Knitting needles

3 ¼ Double pointed needles

Or French Knitting tool 2 ply wool 200 g (any colour)

Oddments of coloured wool 2 ply

Toy stuffing

Round of cardboard for inside base of vase: 7 cm diameter.
Varies lengths wire for the flower stems, 7, 9, 11 inches
Embroidery needle

Abbreviations:
K – Knit,
P – Pearl
Inc – increase
Tog – together
St-st – stocking stitch
St / sts – Stitch-Stitches
Rib stitch (K1, P1) Single knit stitches alternate with single purl stitches, creating very narrow columns

Vase
R0 – Cast on 75 stitches
R1–10; starting with Rib st
R11 – (K1, K2tog to end) (50sts)
R12 – P (P3, P2tog) to end, (40sts)
R13–24 – st-st; starting with P row
R25 – (K7 Inc in next stitch) to end, (45sts)
R26–28 – st-st
R29 – (K8 Inc next stitch) repeat to end, (50sts)
R30–34 – st-st
R35 – (K4 Inc in next st), (repeat to end), K1 (60 sts)
R36–40 – st-st
R41 – (K5 Inc1 in next st to end), (70sts)
R42–50 – st-st
R51 – (K5, K2tog to end), (60sts)
R52–54 – st-st
R55– (K4, K2tog to end), (50sts)

R56–58 – st-st

R59 – (K3, K2tog to end), (40sts)

R60–64 – st-st

R65 – (K6, K2tog to end), (35sts)

R66 – Knit row

R67 – Knit row

R68 – Knit row

R69 – K3, K2tog to end,

R70 – Knit

R71 – K2tog (14sts)

R72 – K2tog, (7sts)

Cut of wool and draw through the stitches and sew up the two sides

Cut out a 7 cm diameter of cardboard to put in the base of the vase and stuff. Shape the vase while putting a little stuffing in at a time. When putting flower in, snip with small scissors in the middle of the stuffing, which will allow you to put the stems in.

Stand

Cast on 12 st

1 – K

2 – P

3 – K

4 – K

5 – cast on first and last st (14sts)

6 – P

7 – cast on first and last st(16sts)

8 – P

9 – K

10 – P

11 – K, cast of first and last st (14sts)
12 – P, cast of first and last st(12sts)
13 – K, cast of first and last st(10sts)
14 – P, cast of first and last(8sts)
15 – Knit 2 tog till end (4st)
14 – draw wool through the sts

Sew up sides, stuff until firm and shape gently. Gather and sew up bottom making against shape.

Using black wool embroider three straight lines in bottom middle of petal; create 5.

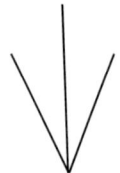

Middle of Flower.
Cast on 8 sts (stocking stitch)
R1 – K

R2 – P

R3 – K, cast on first and last st (10 st)

R4 – P

R5 – K, cast on first and last st (12 sts)

R6 – P

R7 – K, cast of first and last stitch(10sts)

R8 – P

R9 – K, cast of first and last stitch (8 sts)

R10 – P

R11 – draw wool through the sts

Sew up sides; stuff until firm and shape gently; gather all sides and sew up bottom.

Leaf

Cast on 10 st

R1–4 – garter st

R5 – cast on first and last st(12sts)

R6 – GSR7, cast on first and last stitch(14sts)

R8 – GS

R9 – cast on first and last st(16sts)

R10–12 – GS

R13 – cast of first and last st(14sts)

R14 – GS

R15 – cast of first and last st

(12sts)

R16 – GS

R17 – cast of first and last st(10sts)

R18 – GS
R19 – cast of first and last st(8sts)
R20 – GS
R21 – cast of first and last st(6sts)
R22 – GS
R23 – cast of first and last st(4sts)
R24 – GS
R25 – Knit 2tog till end(2sts)
R26 – Knit 2 tog (1 st)
R27 – draw wool through sts
Attach at the back of flower.

Stem

French knitting tool or double-pointed needles; knit preferred size of stem. Push wire through and secure both ends, attach to flower at the back: 7, 9 and 11 inches.

Chapter 10
Flower and Vase 10

6" Tall:

For this project, you will need:
3 ¼ Knitting needles (3 ¼ circular needles and Double pointed needles) Oddments of wool lengths of pipe cleaners, cut into 6-inch lengths
Handful of toy stuffing

4.5 cm diameter round of cardboard

Abbreviations:

K – knit

P – pearl

Inc – increase

Tog – together

sts – stitches

st-st – stocking stitch

Yo – yarn over, wrap yarn around needle

This vase can be made on circular needles. The pearl rows are switched to knit rows. Also keep marker on needle for marking rows. At row 35, switch to double pointed needles.

Vase

To make Vase

Cast on 30 stitches

R1 – Knit row

R2 – Pearl row

R3 – Knit row

R4 – Pearl row

R5 – Knit row

R6 – Pearl row

R7 – K1, K2tog to end (20sts)

R8 – Pearl row

R9 – Knit Row

R10 – Pearl row

R11 – Knit row

R12 – Pearl row

R13 – Knit row

R14 – pearl row

R15 – (k4 inc in next stitch), repeat till end (24sts)

R16 – Pearl row

R17 – Knit row

R18 – Pearl row

R19 – (K5, inc in next stitch) repeat until end (28sts)

R20 – Pearl row

R21 – Knit row

R22 – pearl row

R23 – K4, Inc in next stitch, (K2 Inc in next stitch, repeat 6 times), k4, Inc next stitch (36sts)

R24 – Pearl row

R25 – Knit row

R26 – Pearl row

R27 – k4, k2tog, (K2, K2tog 6 times), K4, k2tog – (28sts)

R28 – Pearl row

R29 – Knit row

R30 – Pearl row

R31 – K3, K2tog, (K1, K2tog, 6 times), K3, K2 tog – (20sts)

R32 – Pearl row

R33 – Knit row

R34 – Pearl row

R35 – K3, K2tog repeat 4 times (16sts)

R36 – Knit row

R37 – Knit row

R38 – Knit row

R39 – K2tog, to end (8sts)

R40 – K2tog, to end (4sts)

R41 – Cut off wool and draw through the stitches; sew upside of vase.

Cut out 5 cm round of cardboard to put in the base of the vase and stuff, making sure you don't overstuff.

For the stand cast on 4sts, use the French knitting tool or double-pointed needles and knit 7 inch long. Attach to bottom of vase.

Ribbon:
R0 – cast on 4sts
R1 – K2 yo K2 tog
R2 – P
Knit 18.5 cm long.
Attach to vase round the neckline

Flower:
R0 – Cast on 10sts
R1 – K
R2 – P
R3 – Inc first and last st(12sts)
R4 – P
R5 – Inc first and last st(14sts)
R6 – P
R7 – cast of first and last st(12sts)
R8 – P
R9 – Cast of first and last st(10sts)
R10 – P

Cut wool and draw through stitches tightly. Sew upside. Put in a little stuffing and sew up bottom gathering tightly.

Press top and bottom together to form bottom shape. Embroider 2 black stitches in the middle, entering from middle back bottom to top and them bottom twice.

Take pipe 6-inch-long cleaner and sew it through the back of the flower.

Make as many as preferred. Then arrange and put in vase. Arrange flowers and twist the pipe cleaners at the bottom to form a stub.

After stuffing the vase, take small scissor and snip in middle of stuffing to make a hole.

This makes easier to place flowers.